Colors

Written and illustrated by Alex Araeipour

www.innovativeinkpublishing.com
Send all inquiries to:
4050 Westmark Drive
Dubuque, IA 52004-1840

Print ISBN: 979-8-3851-0969-2
Ebook ISBN: 979-8-3851-0970-8

Published in the United States of America

This book is dedicated to my son, Alex Araeipour, who inspired me to publish his words of wisdom on his behalf since his passing in 2013. His book "Colors" speaks a universal truth "be proud of who you are" and that being different should be celebrated and embraced. This book is also dedicated to my mother, Marilyn (Harken) Araeipour, who was an early childhood educator and advocate of children. She not only adored Alex and was his biggest fan, she inspired Alex, me, my brothers, her students, and anyone she got to know with her love, compassion, and values of acceptance for diversity for the greater good of human kind.

There are many colors in the world like:
Red
Orange
Yellow
Green
Blue
and
Purple

But some colors did not fit in like Black.
All the other colors were bright and colorful.
No one seemed to notice Black.
He was left all alone so he pouted and felt sorry for himself.
He felt small and unwanted.

He looks funny

Ha Ha

Ha Ha Ha
Ha Ha
Ha

He's ugly

Ha Ha

What kind of color is that!

He wanted to be like all the other colors.
The worst part was they laughed
and made fun of him when they
did notice him.

He was so ashamed that he hid in the dark so no one could see him.
He was hidden for days, weeks, months, and finally a year . . . . . crying.

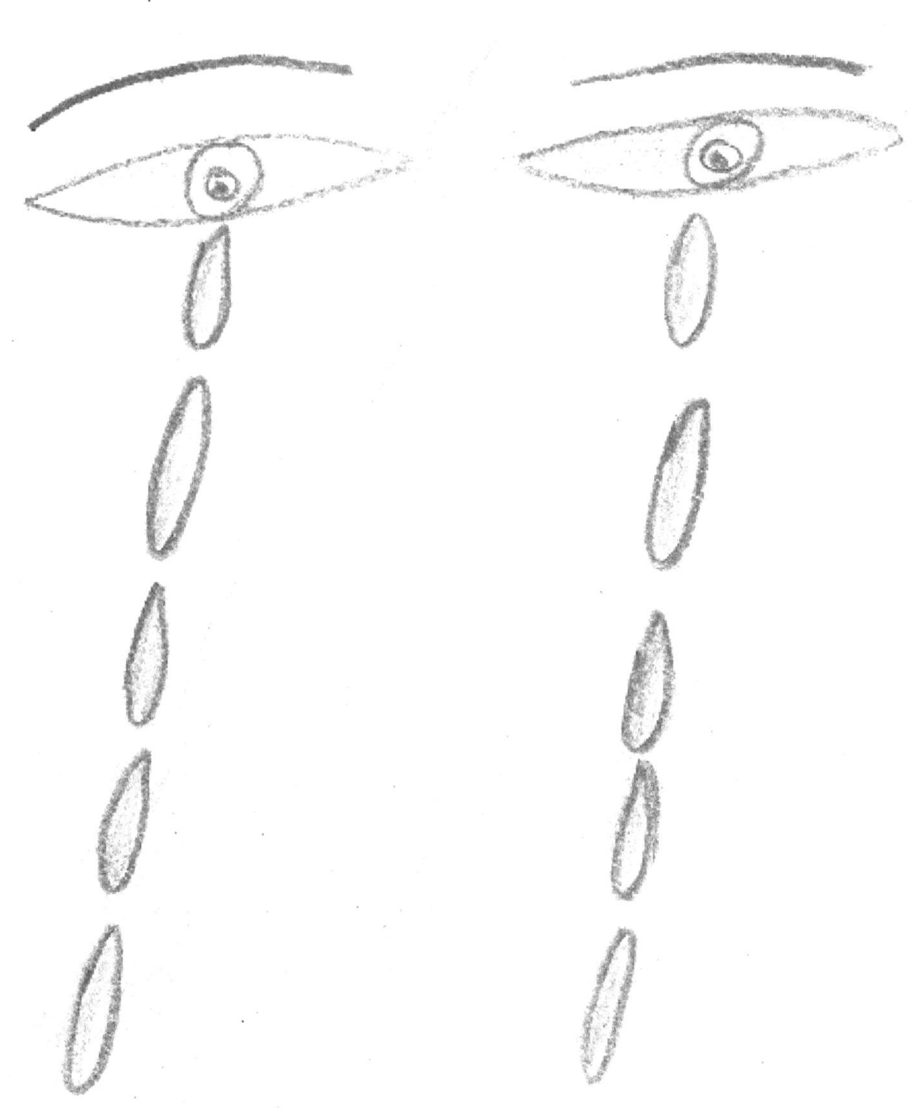

One day a color that he could not make
out asked him what he was doing.
He did not reply.

The color came out of the darkness.
It was Gold!
Black was blinded
yet amazed by her elegant beauty.

She asked him if he would like to be a light color.
He said yes.
She made sure his final answer was yes. Black agreed.
Gold replied, "You make the night I make the light.
You should accept yourself for who you are and don't
be afraid to be different."

Black realized that he should accept himself for who he is not how everyone else wants him to look or be.

He finally fit in.

The End